Cancer Courts My Mother

LindaAnn LoSchiavo

Cancer Courts My Mother

Prolific Pulse Press LLC
Published November 2025
Raleigh, North Carolina USA

ISBN 978-1-962374-64-4 Paperback

ISBN 978-1-962374-65-1 ePub

Cover artist: Erin Caldwell

Dedicated to Philip and Sibylle LoSchiavo

Books by the Author

Conflicted Excitement

A Route Obscure and Lonely

Concupiscent Consumption

Women Who Were Warned

Messengers of the Macabre: Hallowe'en Poems

Vampire Ventures

Apprenticed to the Night

Felones de Se: Poems about Suicide

Always Haunted: Hallowe'en Poems

Cancer Courts My Mother

Vampire Verses

Contents

Acknowledgements

"Arrival"
— in *Big City Lit* (USA)

"Flash"
— in *October Hill Magazine* (USA); rpt in *Querencia Press, Quarterly Anthology* (USA)

"Mother on Morphine, Dreaming of Anna Magnani"
— in *Wax Poetry and Arts* (Canada), Second Place Prize Winner

"Tick Tick"
— in *The Fib Review,* Muse-Pie Press (USA)

"Sickroom at 138 Degrees Fahrenheit"
— in *Hot Pot Magazine* (USA); rpt in *Querencia Press, Quarterly Anthology* (USA)

"Early Visit from the Grim Reaper"
— in *Spectral Realms* (USA); rpt in *BFS Horizons* (England)

"Bartering with Cancer"
— in *The Globe Review* (Hungary)

"Jaundice"
— in *In Parentheses* (USA)

"My Mother's Ghost Dancing"
— in *Choeofpleirn Press* (USA), Finalist; rpt in *Roi Fainéant Press* (USA)

"Cancer, You Sly Casanova"
— forthcoming in *The Listening Eye* (USA)

"Cento: Nightsong for Mother"
    — in *Unlost Journal* (Australia)

"The Closet as She Left it"
    — in *The Remington Review* (USA); rpt in *Months to Years* (USA); rpt in *Loss Lifespan*, Vol. 9, Pure Slush Books (Australia)

Artist Statement

"... every poem breaks a silence that had to be overcome ..."
— Adrienne Rich

Perhaps because I grew up in a Roman Catholic family, I am drawn to acrostics (crosses) and the punitive syllable counting (the rosary) required by formal verse. I often employ traditional forms that harness language and shape unruly thoughts. I use rhyme — both internal and end line — conceding to a self-conscious artifice that rearranges the unfamiliar into something less formidable, i.e., personifying Cancer as my mother's devoted and determined suitor. Everything has a border, the edge where light cannot get in. In this poetry collection, I've tried to illuminate the difficult daily rituals of taking care of a patient who will neither show improvement nor recuperate.

Cancer Courts My Mother

Diagnosis

A diagnosis leads a family on-
Wards, that halo of dark whispers attached. The
Questions, small as seeds, sprout whenever the phone
Rings, until the mind's garden is overrun. Your
Transformation's required, starting with your voice,
Hemorrhaging with euphemisms, lies. You could
Be an actor fed fake dialogue, words almost
A well-rehearsed performance. You could be-
Come an acrobat, clutching the girders of hope. A
Safety net's missing. The laughter is a ghost's.

Source: "For a Teacher's Wife, Dying of Cancer" by Richard
Tillinghast [1966]

Lines used: *On the phone your voice/ Could almost be a
ghost's ...*

Mother Magnified

My mother's lies propelled her life, steered fate towards brittle stars. Truth, like silence, lodged itself like a bone in her throat.

It was my mother who marked the start of when my life was being archived. According to her, everything was my fault. Such distorted recollections became a burden, a sour aftertaste. A child, I sensed danger everywhere as she deftly plucked my words from the air and flung them back at me, keeping a straight face. Sharp was the taste of her rage, the biting sting of blood inside my cheek. The hidden weight of her weather oppressive, my secret self divulged little lest thunderbolts quake.

Eventually, I became a vegetarian, refusing to eat anything that had a mother. The slimmer I got, the more years my mother shaved off, making *herself* younger. An alibi saved for a day of need.

As maturity moved forward, the muscularity of forgetfulness tried to put its seductive palms on my lips and press down. Even imagination threatened to betray me, failing to make good on the fancies I'd hope to invent. But pen and paper became the dependable parents I'd always longed for. With them, I sketched realities I could eventually escape to.

Then along came cancer's onslaught, a beast that called to me like the wilderness summoned the pioneers. From the waiting room, I watched as she was wheeled into a bright cold room on a gurney whose wheels chattered despair. Surgeons promised to extinguish the embers of disease, snuff out its sparks, stamp it out. If the ending was good, it cast its goodness back on the whole like a beautiful sunset's crown after a storm.

Remission repainted the daylight a kinder shade, hinting at a longer stay. But in the rasp of her breathing, death listened for its cue like a stage-door Johnny.

Her final bout with cancer made her reconsider falsehoods that would be etched in tombstone cursive. Framing it as a wish to leave a place where bad luck cursed her, she offered her body to the incinerator, hoping to spell her body into stardust as bald truth, an unruly guest, would be escorted from the premises.

Bad memories are cadavers that refuse burial. Instead of an archive of velveteen nostalgia, her name leaves gravel in my mouth. But there is a dimension where regret might slumber as the sky offers continuity, its sonata of stars promising relief — light's unsingable psalm.

Arrival

Before my father stops hugging me, before he dries his frosted eyes, before he commandeers my suitcase, I know our agendas are beating different drums, his expectations clouded with denial.

Before I arrange her medications, consign the complex sequences of patches, dosages, and Roxanol refills to a spreadsheet, before I gently peek inside the master bedroom, I know *he's* made himself at home, the dark prince whose wanton seduction has already begun, the sly suitor who will reach the terminus first, conveying her silently into his sunless realm.

Before I set about nursing neglected houseplants, manicuring brown-tipped leaves, recovery in my heart, I sense the shush of air-cooled breeze in empty alcoves, Tampa's hopeful blue expanse about to ashen, date palms about to shiver in streetlight, the dusk's fatal crawl towards night.

Terminal Illness

terminal illness
twirls out of the speech of men
exhales rush headfirst

Green Nursemaid

Her plants daydream resuscitation, green ribs nudging each other as I approach, a tarnished brass mister in tow, my face no longer a map of sleeplessness and pique, gambling with fate. Plucking away dead leaves, I debride each dusty surface like a wound, pinch back unruly shoots, inject vitamins, suturing new healthiness into the exhausted potting mixture as deft fingers fly in and out of ceramic pots, a comforting busyness.

If I could always have beauty on hand, would my mother love me?

There comes a chill. From a dark corner, something stirred, glinting faintly in the exodus of grow lights, boastful, staring, puffed with power, the entity I cannot extinguish with insect spray, the cancerous worm inside my stricken mother.

I whisper the word *revive* to my filigreed companions, the exquisite eyelash begonias, and their less showy, leggy neighbors. "Revive," I repeat. Over and over like a spell.

> indoor sun
> last year her voice
> filled this lanai

Flash

To hear my mother tell it, after childbirth her spine rebelled, becoming a cold and rumbling fault line. A difficult breech delivery ruined everything.

To hear my mother tell it, a respectful infant should politely slide from the womb, not unlike a love letter shrugging off its scented pink envelope. But a willful neonate deliberately positions herself awkwardly in the birth canal, taut as a bowstring emerging from its warrior cave of shadows. *En garde.*

To hear my mother tell it, from that point, good health slipped free of her, becoming a fancy hat she never could afford again. Her pre-nuptial decades were later mythologized into a golden era of uncomplicated serenity.

Her lies bore only a passing likeness to reality. Around me, the purifying flames of authenticity were stifled, denuding the landscape of affectionate memories, scorching everything but blame, illusions. Cherishing slipped away like days we couldn't hold onto, truth's mouth sewn shut. We never mastered the mechanics of mother-daughter camaraderie.

My devotion clicked its heels in steady, meaningless rhythm, invisible, buried under her volcanic scorn — until one day nursing was necessary. Cancer helped adorn my mother with patience, her acidic breath pausing to accept the spoon that brought breakfast, her daylight swallowing fast.

Apologies emerged, released like doves. Between us a tight-chested pause exhaled.

Perhaps she had grasped we only love so long.

Eight Weeks Later

morning glories lift
their arms in supplication
doctor prescribes patience

Living through the Dying

Resuscitate the wilted, raise what's close
To death: on their lanai I'm still green
At miracles, surrounded by a sky
Gone cold, thin tendrils, others that curled up
In self-protection, living through dying:
My mother's crown-of-thorns, old hens and chicks,
Impatiens, rosary vines, all consigned.

I'm trusted to recover favorites
Forgotten in ruined grass blades wisped away,
Neglect decreeing green untimely deaths.

Hidden in its high hum of red desire,
An amaryllis, prized, waits, hibernates.

Remembering Remission Christmas

They'd bickered over her like two suitors:
Vitality, her birthright, who had known
My mother well before her married life,
And *Cancer*, who'd mapped out his own terrain,
Unravelled secret strands of resistance,
Until oncologists chased him away.

Remission Christmas reunited us,
Our joy like steam escaping after frost.

I shipped my gifts to Florida ahead:
Biscotti, pignola cookies, torrone
From Little Italy, fine leather goods,
And for her green thumb, a red amaryllis.

But Safety Harbor's Gulf of Mexico,
Producing Christmastime's Cancerian
Heat in December, had confused this bulb.

Amidst the presents and nativity,
Its empty cradle strewn with straw, green life
Ripped up gay mummy wrapping, and tore loose,
Unhampered by its ground like Lazarus
Unbound. My parents, unprepared for ghosts
Of miracles, became unnerved by sounds
Newborn right by their crèche, the fir tree's base,
Invisible and inexplicable

Cancer Courts My Mother

Like faith. Or like remission. After Mass,
They found a determined amaryllis, force
Which sleeps but cannot die, that mother took to heart.

Remission's Like an Extra Holiday

Remission, like grace, is unmerited.
The ghost of cancer's evicted, dispossessed.
Grim forecasts that ate dreams can be edited.

Tampa Bay's mermaids twirled tails, more spirited.
Three oncologists exited stage left.
Remission, like grace, is unmerited.

Woes sprouted wings and fled, discredited,
All red-smeared memories shunned like rude guests,
Grim forecasts, doomed dreams, readily edited.

Palm trees pirouetted, nearly orbited.
Peel the worried world back to life's core: zest.
Remission, like grace, is unmerited.

Prayer candles in her church, for joy, ignited.
The edge of thought, once preoccupied, coos, "Blessed."
Grim forecasts trampling dreams must be edited.

Cancer shuffled off, its powers forfeited.
Again reigns laughter — with no thoughts of *yet*.
Remission, like grace, is unmerited.
Grim forecasts damning dreams look rosy edited.

Fat Tuesday

her pitcher plant
digests flies like raw meatballs
carnevale: waning moon

Mother on Morphine, Dreaming of Anna Magnani

A madman crushed her favorite makeup
To paint my mother's floor. Imagine rouge
On top of powders, scattered door to door.

"I'll clean this up!" I say till she's relieved,
Obedient enough to swallow her
Tart, medicated, Lotos-like ice cream.

She's less combative, calmed by her morphine.
The mind's embrasures, freed from pain's embrace,
Will search for entertainment and escape
Confinement, longing to erase what's real.

Mom's traveling through Tinseltown and Rome
Of sixty years ago, a fond time when
Magnani commandeered "The Rose Tattoo."
Perhaps to mother films were fancy cures.
An audience suspected everything,
Eventually, would turn out just fine.

My mopping scrolls sweet fictions she can screen
Through fantasy, delaying hideous
Mortality, the final credits roll,
When shovels dance and dust returns to dust.

Since Roxanol has brought its soft hammer
To bear on mother's habit of rebuke,
We're playing she's an actress, which helps script
Our mock reality. We call this place
"A dressing room," her home "a trailer" parked
Aside the set. She's idle now because

Cancer Courts My Mother

It's needed — her director will demand
That shot where she looks rested. It's agreed
She'll close her eyes while I beat grief from rugs.

Making a comeback, newly patient, she
Rehearses. It's an unfamiliar role,
With gentle words expressed with self-control,
Extending herself to unseen marquees.

Detecting flickers of excitement keyed
By movie light, I hope there's room for me.

Tick Tick

Her
Plants
Revive.
Mother sleeps
In morphine's embrace.
Cancer, biding his time, taunts me.

Sickroom at 138 Degrees Fahrenheit

The hospice nurse returns my call today.

I sneak the phone outside, hear bright bird sounds,
Malignancy obscured from this angle.

The noonday sun in Florida's fishbowl
Is cooler than my mother's room. Heat clings,
Perpetually pumped to Dantean
Heights by hard-working oxygenators.

Snores greet my cautious footsteps triggering
Childhood fancies: radiators' hot breath
Protecting us from fairytales of snow
Decades before deep damage came to town.

Chores play on loop as mighty machines beep,
My mouth making promises I can't keep.

Early Visit from the Grim Reaper

Amid buffed blackness of the guest room's drapes,
His baritone commanded me to *GO!*
"What's this about?" I want to say. But "No!"
Emerges first. "I'm staying!" There's no cape,
No hood, no scythe. Night hides his shrunken shape,
Revealing just his James Earl Jones audio
Repeating *GO!* Asleep, I'm puzzled, slow
To understand. I rise. There's no escape.

Lost in the territory of morphine,
You turned off your oxygen, approached death's ledge.
Observed by him, I help you breathe again.
His timing's off — though we'll soon reconvene.
A grimace rises from the bedding's edge
As if to say, "Not *now*. I'll tell you *when*."

Bartering with Cancer

When medicine has nothing more to give,
There's only daughters and morphine prescribed
By doctors never seen. She can't describe
Her suffering but seems less combative
Since Cancer came a-courting. He'll forgive
Coy hesitance. All patients yield to bribes
Of pain relief, embrace the death of light.
Seductive, he's marked her as his captive.

Enduring chemo's banishment, he won,
Determined to drag mother from her sun,
Deprive her of the meal of life. I'm stunned.
There must be hide-outs cancer cannot find —
Dice to throw for aliveness or more time.
Rewind, I dare the universe. *Rewind!*

Sickroom Portrait

her defiant hair
thick, auburn, date-night ready
bedside blooms nodding

CANCER

Casanova cancer's dedicated.
Angered by interference, he deceives,
Nursing his patient, embedding toxic
Cells, hidden away like birthday bonbons,
Entering her liver. Lethal embrace.
Rales, crepitations — his deathbed kisses.

Jaundice

Never a gambler, my mother had somehow drawn lots and wound up with him — Cancer — who felt favored by fate. A woman with dimpled opal arms, her sarcasm crackling with static, generous thighs pale as dumplings that he could wither away. Urothelial carcinoma was quick to show the scornful twinkle of his dominance. He sneaked in, like a two-faced suitor of some standing, and took her relentlessly. A quiet violation.

One morning when the crown-of-thorns revealed a bit of chaste pinking, I waltzed it into the bedroom to provoke her smiles. Her skin had turned sallow, jaundiced.

A shadow hushed the room to silence, chilling in its "cat licking the cream" triumph. During their last rendezvous, his sinister seeds had penetrated her liver. Overnight he claimed his prize. No longer would she speak, a mere vassal now in the palace of death.

Intrusive Music

He's intrusive, the worst kind of pest.

Night after mortal night, he waits
As winds drum an elegy,
Blue music of exile,
Grave language of loss.

His theme song plays —
Will not stop.

It's her
Dirge.

My Mother's Ghost Dancing

That year morphine became a minuet,
Sweet pianissimo. Its soft pedals stilled
Anguish, reproached relentless timekeeping —
Tick, tick — mortality's metronome.

Before my mother died at home, she learned
That cancer's like a Depression Era
Endurance contest: the dance marathon,
Odds stacked against her, swaying in slow mode.

Despite defiant hair, a plump physique
Deceiving guests, illness hokey-pokeyed
Her organs, shook breasts off, rhumbaed her cells,
Vitality an unremembered song,
Mere noise until sweet exhalations ceased.

Her corpse was wheeled away. The tempo changed.

Dynamic force reclaimed the rooms, infirm
No longer. Energy expressed intent
As if Mom were at a debutante's ball,
Star of the floor show, sequined, applauded.

The mind's embrasures, freed from pain's embrace,
Seek entertainment, longing to erase
What's real. Belonging to another realm —
Where everyone's transparent — Mom's got plans
She's telepathed. But first she wants to dance.

A coldness sidles up to seize my hand.

Cancer, You Sly Casanova

Grief wrung our door, its last drops of woe spent,
Allowing me an about-face from bold
Audacity, its feathers set on fire
Before evolving into ash and rue.

Cancer's devotion — all consuming — trumped
My ministrations, rooting deeper as
Resistance weakened. Mother fought him off,
Insisting she was married to her life,
Unwilling to abandon family
And friends for his seductive promises
Of peace, relief from pain. Disease does not
Relax dark efforts. Like a gigolo,
He teased, urging mother to succumb.

He ransacked her impatient body till
She was persuaded to leave us for him,
Not realizing all Casanovas
Are interested only in conquest.

Nightsong for Mother

Mother, dying — mother not wanting to die.
The mother says, I am afraid.
Mother's sitting on the bed with her tattered list of
dispersals — who gets what.
Machine of the mother: white city inside her.

When my mother died, she took home along with her.

Grief has its own gravity.

Something is dancing on leaf drift, dancing across the
graves.

— Cento sources —

Line 1: "Mother's Hands Drawing Me" by Jorie Graham, 2016.
Line 2: "Mother and Daughter" by Hayan Charara, 2016.
Line 3: "Mother's Closet" by Maxine Scates, 2005.
Line 4: "Mother and Child" by Louise Glück, 2001.
Line 5: "My Mother Died with Her Home" by Temidayo Jacob, 2019.
Line 6: "Letter to My Mother, One Year After Her Death" by Megan Merchant, 2019.
Line 7: "Mother Garden's Round" by Muriel Rukeyser, 1955.

Mother Requests Miracles

My mother, worried her plants wouldn't thrive,
Consigned this large green fellowship, orphaned,
Underprivileged guests, despondency
On wilted stalks, to me — the chosen one.
An African violet row revealed
Brown-tinged dismay on fuzzy leaves devoid
Of rosy cheer. Anemic ivy sulked
From hanging cradles, droopy with despair.
Witness to agony, the crown-of-thorns
Questioned my late-stage intercession here.

"Work miracles," commanded half-shut eyes.

Doubts? Pursed lips will be a casket for them.

Like Juliet, leaves beckoned from the sill,
Insisting — in their ancient argot —
They come in peace, meek seeking nourishment,
Unlike rude, uninvited cancer, growth
Emboldened — deep roots sealing hope's mouth shut.

Hydration occupied me, drizzling her
Dose dutifully on a squirming tongue.
Parched plants await the water jar, blue-green
With vitamins, recovery in sight.

Worming into her worn out cardigan,
Penning a eulogy, my hands perspire.

Fronds dance, sweet partnered with the breeze, remind
Me, in their voiceless joy, I'm not alone.

The Closet as She Left It

Deprived by his wife's absence, grieving guts
My father. The cremation over now,
Her ashes urned and glowing with repose,
Inspection of her closet is the next
Unmaking, contents intimate, perfumed.

Attired in nightgowns longer than a year,
My mother needed nothing stored inside:
Complacent church clothes, pastel linen sheaths,
Insomniacal sling-back heels, upright,
Attentive, waiting for the toll of tread,
Accessories forgotten, unloved, cold.

Sharp hangers await uninvited guests,
Prepared to scar. Should caretakers encroach,
Conspirators rise: boucle knits scratching,
Steel eye-hooks, belts resisting, stuffy air
Redolent of her scent almost forcing
The trespasser to leave belongings there,
Mourned privately by what caressed her skin,
The nude audacity of death dismissed
As long as things remain, her door pulled shut.

Bio

LindaAnn LoSchiavo

Native New Yorker and award-winner, LindaAnn LoSchiavo is a member of British Fantasy Society, Horror Writers Association, Science Fiction Poetry Association, and The Dramatists Guild.

Her craft essays have appeared in *Writer's Digest, Authors Publish Magazine, Beyond Craft, Behind the Pages, Roi Fainéant,* and elsewhere.

Between 2018-2025, she has had nine chapbooks and two full-length collections released by various presses.

Book Accolades: Elgin Award for "A Route Obscure and Lonely"; Chrysalis BREW Project's Award for Excellence and The World's Best Magazine's Book of Excellence Award for "Always Haunted: Hallowe'en Poems"; and the Spotlyts Story Award from *Spotlyts Magazine* for "Apprenticed to the Night." Additionally, "Always Haunted: Hallowe'en Poems" achieved recognition as a 3rd Place Finalist in Chrysalis BREW Project's Readers' Choice Awards, 2024-2025.

BlueSky: @ghostlyverse.bsky.social

www.ingramcontent.com/pod-product-compliance
Lightning Source LLC
Chambersburg PA
CBHW020812130626
46554CB00006B/2404